# LAUGHTER
## on the
# Level

## MARTIN FAULKS

Lewis Masonic

Laughter on the Level
**Martin Faulks**

First published 2012

ISBN 978 0 85318 404 1

Published by Lewis Masonic

an imprint of Ian Allan Publishing Ltd, Hersham, Surrey KT12 4RG.
Printed in England by Ian Allan Printing Ltd, Hersham, Surrey KT12 4RG.

Visit the Lewis Masonic website at www.lewismasonic.com

Distributed in the United States of America and Canada by BookMasters Distribution Services.

**Picture Credits:** Illustrations by Steve Chadburn

Dedicated to my dear friend Yasha Beresiner,
who taught me that there is far more to
Masonic charity than just giving money.

Q:   How many Freemasons does it take to change a light bulb?
A:   It's a secret.

•

Q:   How many Freemasons does it take to change a light bulb?
A:   Three. One to screw it in, one to read the minutes of the previous light bulb replacement, and one to complain that this wasn't the way they USED to screw in light bulbs.

•

A man says to his mate –
"I'm getting really fed up with my old tom cat; every time I go out into the garden there are loads of female cats around him and the noise from them at night is keeping me awake." His pal said: "Then you want to get him doctored; that will keep the other cats away." This he promptly did. Then one morning he got up and there on a branch of a large tree in the garden was his old tom surrounded by a line of female cats. On seeing his friend again he immediately started to tell him off, saying: "I thought you said that would clear up the problem, which it clearly hasn't!" to which his friend answered:

"HE MIGHT HAVE LOST HIS TOOLS OF OFFICE BUT
HE CAN STILL HOLD LODGE OF INSTRUCTION."

•

Q:   How many Freemasons does it take to change a light bulb?
A:   Twenty, as follows:
     Two to complain that the light doesn't work.
     One to pass the problem to the Master of the Lodge.
     Three to do a study on the light in the Lodge.
     Two to check out the types of lights the Knights of Columbus use.
     Five to plan a fund-raising dinner to raise money for the replacement bulb.
     Three to argue over it.
     Two to complain that "It's not the way we did it before".
     One to borrow a ladder, donate the bulb and install it
     One to order the brass 'light bulb memorial plate' and have it inscribed.

•

4

Q:     How many Freemasons does it take to change a light bulb?
A:     Three and a chair.
       You need one Worshipful Master and two Wardens. The Worshipful
       Master stands on the chair, puts the light bulb in the socket and the
       Wardens turn the chair to help him screw it in.

Q:    How many Past Masters does it take to change a light bulb?
A:    Change it? Why?

A newly made Freemason is sitting at the festive board talking to the Worshipful Master. The Worshipful Master asks him if he understands what all the Lodge Officers' jobs are. The newly made Mason responds:

"Well, I know what your job is and I understand what the two men sitting in the other seats did. I can understand why the men on the outside and inside work together to guard the door. However, I have one question.

'Who was that nasty rude man who walked around with me and kept interrupting all the time?'"

"That would be the Junior Deacon," said the Worshipful Master.

Q:  Why was King Solomon so wise?
A:  Because he had 500 wives to tell him what to do!

•

**The Working Tools of the Festive Board. . .**
I now present to you the working tools of the Festive Board.

They are the Knife, the Fork, the Goblet and the Common Gabble.

The Knife is to cut off all knobs and etceteras from anything edible, digestible or comestible and so to render it fit for the jaws of the expert workman.

The Fork is intended to convey the materials so prepared and is placed between the two rows of pillars situated at the porch way or entrance somewhat below the temple. You will notice, Brethren, that the Fork has several points or prongs. At first all are disclosed, but soon all are hidden, and the number of times this is done to the minute denotes the progress you are making in the science.

The Goblet is to hold what the Stewards feel disposed to contribute, which will be thankfully received and faithfully applied. It is only to be used when there is one, and only one, Worshipful Master of the Lodge present. If you see two, then you are making too much progress in the science.

The Common Gabble is used to cheer and edify the workmen whilst waiting for material; also for ornamenting, adorning, embroidering and embellishing our speech, so that as members we may say of our Worshipful Master and Officers, however they work, "Oh Wonderful Masons".

The peculiar sign of this degree is called the ailing sign or sign of repletion. It is given by a distinctive pressure on the last two buttons of the waistcoat and denotes 'plenty'.

But as we are not all operative Masons, but sometimes very speculative Masons, we apply these tools to our morals. In this sense, the Knife teaches us to keep our portions in due bounds and the Fork teaches us to estimate and determine the limits and capacity of our distended structure. The Goblet makes us all tell the truth with a freedom and expression that is at once surprising and illuminating, whilst the Common Gabble tells us the value of goodwill, kindness and friendship.

Thus, let our Knives be cutting, but not our Gabble; our Forks held in check, but not our digestions; and our Goblets filled with the spirit of brotherhood and benevolence. And moreover Brethren, whilst at the beginning we pay respect to the Crown let us not fail to deposit our appreciation with the Tyler ere we depart.

•

**The Working Tools of a Visiting Mason**
They are the working Knife, the Fork and the Goblet. The Knife is an implement which acts with the fork whence a cut is drawn through the meat, fish or poultry. The Fork marks out the intended vegetables which are needed and conveys them pure and unsullied to the beholder. The Goblet is a tool with which the skilful Steward tries and adjusts the right amount of wine required.

But as we are often visiting Masons we sometimes apply these tools to our table manners, in this sense. The Knife is often used to emphasise a point of conversation. The Fork with its four points reminds us of the four points of Fellowship which I am sure we extend to our guests tonight. The Goblet is raised to wish the Health and Happiness to all our visitors.

•

A Tyler salutes with his sword.
One Brother said: "You missed me!"
"Just wait until you nod," said the Tyler.

•

Some people think that Masonic ritual is a matter of life and death.
I can assure you it's far more important than that!

•

A young Mason to the Director of Ceremonies: "What do you get for becoming Master of a Lodge?"

DC: "A Past Master's apron, a Past Master jewel and an extra five inches on your waist measurement." (Those who have been there will understand.)

•

A group of Masons are sitting around the festive board. One pipes up, saying:

"I once visited a Lodge in Yorkshire that all wore tricorn hats."

"That's nothing," says another Brother, "I visited a Lodge in Cambridge that all wore special Masonic suits."

"I can beat that," said one old Brother. "I visited a military Masonic Lodge that met in a submarine. The Tyler had to wear a frog suit."

Once upon a time an English Mason was visiting a Masonic Lodge in China. However, he didn't know any Chinese, so he was understandably worried when he was asked to do the response on behalf of the guests.

"What shall I do?" he asked his English-speaking host.

"Just stand up, bow to the Worshipful Master, bow to the Senior Warden and then the Junior Warden," answered his host. So he stood up, bowed to the Worshipful Master, bowed to the Senior Warden and then bowed to the Junior Warden. The response was a thunderous applause. So he did it again! He bowed to the Worshipful Master, bowed to the Senior Warden and then bowed to the Junior Warden. This time everyone booed.

"What did I do wrong?" he asked upon sitting down.

"You went on too long," said his host.

•

Q:    What do you call a porcupine with an apron on?
A:    Ma-Sonic the Hedgehog!

•

A gentleman is walking his dog through his local park when he notices a rather frantic and disorganised football match taking place on the park's football pitch.

"What's going on?" he asks a spectator who is watching from the sidelines. The other replies: "It's a match between the Masons and the Odd Fellows."

"What's the score?" asks the first man.

"I don't know," says the spectator, "it's a secret."

•

A Grand Officer was attending a meeting at Great Queen Street and as he arrived outside the entrance to the building he saw a rather dishevelled fellow sitting at the side of the road with a fishing rod.

The rod was directed with line, hook and bait toward the centre of the road. Remembering his obligation and the need for charity our Brother pressed a pound coin into the hand of the angler with the wish for him to use it to gain food and drink.

Prior to entering the Temple he inquired of the man as to how many he had caught that day.

"Well, you're the ninth!" was the firm reply!

•

A local Lodge member was called to an interview with the Senior Tax Inspector. At the Lodge meeting he asked a Brother who was an accountant for his advice on what to wear. "Wear your shabbiest clothing. Let him think you are pauper," the accountant Brother replied.

Then he asked another Brother, who was a lawyer, the same question, but got the opposite advice. "Don't let them intimidate you. Wear your most elegant suit and tie."

Confused, the man went to the Director of Ceremonies, told him of the conflicting advice, and requested some resolution of the dilemma.

"Let me tell you a story," replied the DC.

"A woman, about to be married, asked her mother what to wear on her wedding night. "Wear a heavy, long, flannel nightgown that goes right up to your neck.'

"But when she asked her best friend, she got conflicting advice. 'Wear your most sexy negligee, with a V neck right down to your navel.'"

"What does all this have to do with my problem with the Tax Inspector?" the confused Brother asked.

The DC replied, "No matter what you wear, you are going to get screwed."

•

"To do
is to be."
— Plato

"To be
is to do."
— Kant

"Do be
do be do."
— Sinatra

•

One day a Lodge Secretary received a rather worrying phone call from the wife of a newly initiated Brother.

"I don't know what's wrong with him," she complained. "He has started behaving very strangely since joining Masonry."

"In what way?" enquired the Secretary.

"Well," said the wife, "he locks himself in the bathroom for hours on end, mumbling to himself with his strange little blue book."

"Don't worry, I'll have a word with him," the Secretary replied in a reassuring manner.

Later that evening at the festive board the Secretary had a chance for a quiet word with the Brother in question.

"I understand that you need to learn your lines but why do you have to do it in there?" he asked.

"Well," said the newly made Brother. "It's the only TYLED room in the house . . ."

•

During one particularly hot English summer evening, in the baking heat, a Lodge had a bit of bad luck. It was preparing to initiate a candidate and the air conditioner had stopped working. After sweating their way through part of the ritual, the Master asked the candidate: ". . . having been kept in a state of darkness, what, in your present situation, is the predominant wish in your heart?"

The candidate replied: "A beer."

At this juncture the WM, being startled, whispered "light", to the candidate.

"OK," the candidate replied, "a lite beer."

•

The Worshipful Master of a Lodge is woken in the night by drunken singing in the street outside his house. As he rises to give the singer a piece of his mind, he realises he recognises the voice as that of the Lodge Junior Deacon. So he leans out of his bedroom and sure enough he sees the Junior Deacon staggering down the street in a drunken manner.

"Brother! Where are you going at this time of night in that state?" he demands.

"Il'mm on mmyy waayyy . . . to a lectttuurre . . . on Ffreemmassonnrrry," replies the JD.

The WM is puzzled and says: "I can tell by the state of you that you have been to a Lodge meeting already. Where can you possibly get a lecture on Freemasonry at this time of night?"

JD: "Frromm mmyy wifffe, wwhenn I gget homme!"

•

On the night of his initiation, one poor candidate got into his car to drive to the temple, when the car broke down. Not having time to fix the car or even identify the problem, the candidate decided to ride to Lodge on his bicycle.

His bad luck continuing, halfway through the journey, at the top of a large hill, his chain broke! As the Lodge was at the bottom of the other side of the hill all he needed was the back-pedal brake, so he repaired the chain with a cord he had in his pocket and freewheeled downhill to the Lodge.

Later that evening, in reply to a toast in his honour, he said how proud he was to be a Freemason but could not understand, as he had not told anyone, how the WM knew that he had come on his own free wheel and a cord.

●

An elderly Mason was in such a hurry to get to his Lodge that when he arrived and sat down, he suddenly realised that he had forgotten his false teeth. Turning to the visitor next to him he said, "I forgot my teeth, and I'm supposed to be giving an explanation of the tracing board."

The visitor said, "I see your problem, but perhaps I can help." With that, he reached into his pocket and pulled out a pair of false teeth. "Try these," he said.

The old man tried them. "Too loose," he said.

The visitor then said, "I have another pair. . . try these."

The old man tried them and responded, "Too tight."

The visitor was not taken back at all. He then said, "I have one more pair of false teeth. . . try them."

The old man said, "They fit perfectly."

The Lodge work duly completed, the Brethren retired to the festive board.

After the meal, the old man went over to thank the visitor who had come to his assistance in true Masonic fashion.

"Brother, I want to thank you for coming to my aid. Where is your surgery? I've been looking for a good dentist." The visitor replied, "No thanks are necessary Brother, but I'm not a dentist. I'm an undertaker."

●

Bro Andrew and Bro Mike are in the robing room getting ready for a Lodge meeting. When Andrew opens his case to take out his apron, Mike notices a pair of silk stockings neatly rolled up in the corner of the case.

Mike asks: "Andrew, what's this with the ladies clothing in your case?"

Andrew gives a sideways glance and whispers: "You remember the installation meeting last year?"

Mike acknowledges and Andrew goes on: "Keep it to yourself, but on the way home I stopped off at a pub where I met a beautiful lady. Apparently, she lost her stockings in my car and my wife found them. I told my wife I was passed to a higher degree and, ever since, she takes them out of the case, washes them and puts them back in with my gloves!"

David and Derek had been members of the same Lodge for many years. They promised each other that the first of them to pass to the Grand Lodge above would return to tell the other whether there really was Freemasonry in Heaven, and if so what it was like. By and by, as fate would have it, it was Derek who went first.

One day, on his way to Lodge, David heard a whispering voice from the ether. "David! It's me!" He looked around but saw nothing.

A few moments later he heard the same voice again, now quite clearly: "David! It's me, Derek!"

"Derek!" David exclaimed. "Are you in Heaven?"

"Yes I am," said Derek.

David took a few moments to regain his composure. "Well, Derek, are there Lodges up there in Heaven?"

"There certainly are, David. Wonderful Lodges everywhere and they are quite magnificent, far better than anything in Great Queen Street. The meetings are well attended, the ritual is word perfect, the festive board fantastic, the spirit of Freemasonry is all-pervasive and everyone gets on."

"My goodness, Derek," said David. "It certainly sounds very impressive. Tell me, are you having a good time?"

"Well, David, I have some good news and some bad."

"OK, so what's the good news?"

"The good news is that we are doing a Third this Thursday."

"Great," said David. "What's the bad news, then?"

"I just got the summons through and you're the Senior Deacon!"

•

Just before a Lodge is about to open, an ancient-looking man approaches the Tyler. "Ready," he says. "What for?" says the Tyler.

"I'm ready to be passed to the Second Degree."

A complete silence emanates as all the assembled Masons just stare at the old man in confusion.

"I was initiated on December the 12th, 1913. Now I'm ready for my Second Degree."

So the Secretary looks through the records only to find that the elderly man is telling the truth.

"Where have you been all these years? What took you so long to be ready for your Passing?" they ask.

He replies: "As it said in the Ritual, I was learning to subdue my passions!"

•

An elderly Mason who passed away, went to Heaven and met with St Peter. He identified himself as a Freemason to St Peter, who asked him: "What Lodge?"

"Cabbell Lodge, Number 807," he answered proudly.

"Well," said St. Peter, "this might be of interest to you."

He took the Mason to a Heavenly Lodge room. Inside, the never-ending walls were filled with clocks. Each clock had a Lodge's name on a brass plate below it and each clock showed a different time. The Mason asked why and St Peter informed him that the hands moved only when someone in that Lodge made a mistake in the Ritual. After looking for a while, the man asked:

"Why can't I see the clock for my Lodge?"

St Peter replied: "Why, it's in the kitchen, of course."

"The kitchen?" said the Mason.

"Yes," smiled St Peter, "you see, we needed a new fan."

•

After his initiation a newly made Mason returns home. As I am sure you can imagine, his wife is naturally curious to know what happened. The conversation goes something like this:

She: "Well, how'd it go?"

He: "Very well — very interesting."

She: "What happened?"

He: "I can't really tell you about it."

She: "Well, is there anything you can tell me?"

He: "Well it seems there are three types of men in the Lodge — walkers, talkers and holy men."

She: "What do they do — if you can tell me?"

He: "The walkers walked me around the Lodge. The talkers talked to me and to the walkers as I was led around . . ."

She: ". . . and the holy men? What of them?"

He: "They seem to be a special class of men — all in dark blue aprons. They just sit on the benches around the Lodge with their heads in their hands, chanting repeatedly: 'Oh My God! Oh My God!'"

•

A dedicated Freemason came under fire at home one day after he had been visiting too many Lodges.

His wife said to him: "All those Masters-in-office have to do is click their fingers and you would be there, wouldn"t you? . . I wish I was a Master!"

"So do I, dear," he retorted. "We swap those every year!"

•

A senior retired Mason decided to visit the Social Security office to sign up for his benefits. Upon his arrival the clerk asked for proof of his age. When he reached for his wallet, the embarrassed man realised he had left it home. After explaining his problem to the clerk, she replied, "Don't worry, just open your shirt, and if your chest hair is grey you will qualify." The senior citizen opened up his shirt and was soon signed up for his benefits.

Upon arriving home, he related the story to his wife. She looked at him, smiled and said, "Too bad you didn't drop your pants. You would have qualified for disability too!"

•

One evening after a particularly festive, festive board, one Brother had partaken of too much wine. The Worshipful Master was very worried. He did not want the Brother to drive home in his present state of intoxication as he lived some distance away. So he insisted that the Brother stay the night at his house and travel home the next morning. After much persuasion, this is what he did.

When he got home the next morning, his wife was furious with him because he had forgotten to phone. She did not believe his story about staying with a Brother because of the state he had been in, but was worried he had been with another woman. However, she pretended to believe him by asking how the ceremony had gone, how many other Brethren had been there and all the regular questions that wives ask. So he told her that it had been an excellent Lodge meeting and that 55 Brethren had attended.

At the next Lodge meeting, when the Secretary rose to read out correspondence, he read a letter from the wife asking if the Brother with whom her husband had stayed the night after the last Lodge meeting would please write to her and confirm his story.

The next day she received 54 letters in the post.

•

## The Working Tool of an E-Mason
I now present to you the Working tools of an e-Mason.

They are: The Mouse. . .The Keyboard. . .and The Modem.

The Mouse is to move within the desktop, the Keyboard to input the data, and the Modem to publish the data to cyberspace. However, as we are not here assembled as Computer Nerds, but rather as Operative e-Masons, to us these tools are downloaded as vehicles of moral significance and to show us the meaning of e-Masonry. And thus we apply them:

The Mouse teaches us to keep within the bounds of the screen - a square upon which we must all meet.

The Keyboard is to show us that communication will lead us to a better understanding of each other and the rest of mankind.

And the Modem is to remind us that even when we are alone on the most remote part of the globe, we may meet and gain moral sustenance from each other and thus learn more of the wonderful works of the G.A.O.T.U.

•

Tony and Terry were on their way home from a Rose Croix meeting. Tony was giving Terry a lift. He shouldn't have been driving, however, because he was a bit tipsy.

When the traffic cop pulled them over they hoped that he would be a Mason and let them off!

'Racing home are we, sir?" said the policeman. "Michael Schumacher are we, sir?"

At this point Terry noticed that the policeman was wearing a square and compasses lapel pin. Terry whispered to Tony:

"He doesn't know you're a Mason! Show him your cross!"

Tony shouted: "Why don't you piss off and leave us alone?"

•

One day, whilst walking past a Masonic regalia shop, one of two friends noticed an advert in the window: "Masonic Parrots for Sale."

Curiosity made them enter the shop and enquire: "What is this Masonic Parrot advert all about?"

The shopkeeper immediately showed them through to the back room where, on a tall perch, was a parrot, light blue in colour. "That's a Master Parrot. He can recite all Three Degrees word perfectly," he said.

"How much?" they asked.

"£10,000," the shopkeeper replied.

"That's a lot of money," the first friend retorted. "Have you any other parrots?"

"Yes," said the shopkeeper. He went in the back and returned with a magnificent dark blue parrot. "This is a Provincial Grand Parrot," he said. "It can recite all Three Degrees and all the addresses in the back of the book that no one ever looks at, word perfect. He will cost you £25."

"Blimey!" said the friend. "Have you anything cheaper?"

The shopkeeper disappeared again and returned with a slightly scruffy old bird in dark blue but with gold braid down its wings and tail. "This is a Grand Parrot," he said. "He is only ten quid."

"What does he do?" the men asked.

"Nothing. He just sits there shaking his head and going 'Tut, tut . . . tut, tut'."

•

Adam was walking around the Garden of Eden feeling very lonely, so God asked Adam, "What is wrong with you?"

Adam said he didn't have anyone to talk to.

God said he was going to give him a companion and it would be a woman.

He said, "This person will cook for you and wash your clothes, she will always agree with every decision you make. She will bear your children and never ask you to get up in the middle of the night to take care of them. She will not nag you and will always be the first to admit she was wrong when you've had a disagreement. She will never have a headache and will freely give you love and passion whenever needed."

Adam asked God, "What will a woman like this cost?"

God said, "An arm and a leg."

Adam said, "What can I get for just a rib?"

The rest is history.

•

### RAGS TO RICHES
Two tramps who hailed from Rowton House, in nearby Parker Street,
The first consuming rancid bread, the second tasty meat;
Then washed it down with Beaujolais and cool and calmly said:
"I must light up a Davidoff before I go to bed!"

The first tramp could no longer bear the sight of all this wealth,
He laid a plan to learn much more, with cunning and with stealth.
"Where does you get that style 'o life you regarly enjoy?
Fa pete's sake won't ya tell me, you luvly little boy."

"I gets it in Great Queenie Street, I'm tellin' you no lies,
That great big place aruhnd the bend, from geezers wiv black ties.
I goes an' stands outside da door and simply 'angs aruhnd,
Until some likely geezer gives at least a pahnd."

"I tells him I'm a Mason man who's poor and much distressed.
They comes across wiv lots-a-dosh, a coupla pahnd at best."

Our shabby hero, not deterred, decides to do the same,
To pose as if a Brother he, in jest if not in name.
An hour passed without result and then he staggers back
E'en more dishevelled than before, his eye a shiny black.

"What 'appened?" asked his trusty pal, "Where did you get that eye?"
"I git it from a Mason man, who was a passerby.
He asked me what came after "BOW"... An' I said MILE END ROAD...
And then he flamin' hit me, you double dealin' toad!"

•

A newly made Worshipful Master was walking along at the seaside when he found a bottle with a Genie in it. "I am the Genie of the bottle and I will grant you one wish," said the Genie.

"Not three wishes?" said the WM.

"No, just the one," said the Genie.

"OK," thought the newly made Master, "I will wish for something that is of benefit both to myself and Freemasonry in general. Something that benefits us all."

So he says to the Genie, "I've always wanted to go to America to see how Freemasonry is done there but I am scared to fly. So my wish is for you to build a bridge between Britain and America. That way both English and American Masons can drive over and visit each other whenever they like!"

"What?" exclaimed the Genie. "How can you expect me to do that? Think of the materials that would be needed! Do you know how deep the water is in that ocean? Have you thought how far it is? Don't you know that's impossible? No one could do that, not even a Genie. You will have to make another wish."

"OK," said the Master. "I wish that throughout the world Freemasonry works how it should. I wish that all the Freemasons get on and that the Past Masters stop 'tutting' and criticising. I wish that the rituals all go well and that the candidates learn from the rituals and apply the meanings and lessons to their lives. I wish that every festive board is fun and that everybody's speeches are short and to the point."

"Hmmmmm," said the Genie after some thought. "Do you want that bridge with two lanes or four?"

•

One poor Brother is driving home from Lodge through central London and finds himself in desperate need to urinate. He looks everywhere for a place to park but every street is covered in double yellow lines. Eventually he gives up and parks on the double yellows next to a public toilet. Needless to say, as soon as he parks a traffic warden appears.

Hoping the traffic warden is a Bro, the Mason pulls out his driving licence and puts it in his ritual book and hands it to the traffic warden, who fails to bat an eyelid.

"Officer," he says, "if you don't mind I am going to park here just for a second or two. I must just restore myself to my personal comforts."

"Right you are, sir,' said the traffic warden, "and on your return, I shall call your attention to a charge."

•

Three men were travelling by train. A little way into the journey, they realised that they were all Masons. The first said, "Well, I've had a good life, I'm a Provincial Officer, I'm happily married and I've got three sons, they're all Doctors and all Master Masons." The second said, "There's a coincidence, I'm a Provincial Officer, I'm happily married and I've got three sons; they're all Chemists and all Master Masons." The third said "Well that's unbelievable, such a coincidence. I'm just a Master Mason, I've never been married but I've got three sons and they're all Provincial Officers!"

•

Boy to Mum: "Mum, how do buffaloes make love?"
Mum: "I don't know, ask your Dad. He's a Mason."

•

At the monthly Masonic Building Society meeting much discussion raged about the problem of mice in the Lodge building. Of course several suggestions on how to be rid of them were offered — set mouse-traps; lay mouse poison; call an exterminator; buy a cat etc. The building manager took all this advice under consideration and it was agreed that at the next meeting he would make a report on his progress. Sure enough, at the next meeting he was questioned. "Did you use my idea of a cat?" "Did you use poison or traps?" Finally, he said: "All the mice are gone." Everyone wanted to know how he had accomplished such a feat.

"Well . . ." he said, "I initiated all the mice into my Lodge and I haven't seen one attend since!"

•

## J.D.'s Lament
*(Author unknown but in the style of Pam Ayres)*
Oh! I wish I'd looked after me Ritual,
I wish I had studied the book,
I might have got through a few meetings,
Without having to take a sly look
At the words printed all neat and tidy
With capital letters and dots
And inverted commas and rows of small hammers
To remind you about them there knocks.

If I'd attended a Lodge of Instruction
And followed the preceptor's plan,
My signs might be more like a Mason and less like a tic tac man.
For a Past Master once said with sarcasm,
As he doffed his apron of blue,
You lay five to one, when the lodge is begun,
And evens the field when it's through.

Time was, when I was a Deacon,
I was proud of me Wand and me Dove.
Initiation was due, and I was in a right stew,
So I wrote all me words on me glove.
Now some candidates are cool and collected,
But mine he was nervous and hot.
I don't mean to boast, but his hand was like toast
Left me palm an illegible blot.

As I thumped the Warden's shoulder,
The ink stained his coat a bright blue,
He said "Who have you there," I stood in despair,
He could see I hadn't a clue.
I gazed at me glove for an answer
At those five fickle fingers of fate'
Then the blots rolled away, left the words plain as day
ST MICHAEL . . . ALL COTTON . . . SIZE EIGHT.

•

A newly raised Brother is discussing his membership with a Proposer. He tells him that, though he's really enjoying his Masonry, it is causing problems with his wife.

"When I come home from a Lodge meeting, I try to be very quiet. I close the front door carefully behind me, lock it with the utmost stealth, take off my shoes and tiptoe upstairs. I get undressed in the dark, pee quietly and don't flush the loo. However, whatever I do, my wife wakes up and is very angry that her sleep has been disturbed. Then we go into a large argument about what time I get in from Lodge."

"I have the solution," says the more experienced Brother. "Do the opposite. Come in loudly, slam the door, stomp upstairs, and shout 'I'm home dear and I'm in the mood for some sexy loving!' I absolutely guarantee she'll be fast asleep before you reach the bedroom."

•

Recently an English Lodge had a visit from a French Lodge and after the Lodge proceedings they all retired to the festive board. The French Director of Ceremonies was seated next to the English DC and conversation about all things ensued. The English DC was particularly impressed by the well-spoken English of the French Brother and decided that he should at least attempt some conversation in the other's tongue.

Just then a fly alighted on the table and the English DC, pointing to the fly, remarked: "Regarde le mouche!"

"Ah!" said our continental Brother, "LA mouche, the fly is female."

At the next Lodge Committee Meeting the DC summing up the visitation said: "Well, I was particularly taken by the French DC's command of English, but what impressed me even more was his fantastic eyesight!"

•

While paying a visit to North Wales, I was about five hours too early for the meeting. Going into the local pub, which was next door to the Masonic Hall, I was invited to take one of their guide dogs, which would lead me on a tour of the local beauty spots.

Of the three presented I chose the DC dog, which was reputed to know everywhere and everything. And he certainly did — he was absolutely excellent. Upon revisiting the area, many months later, I took advantage of the same offer, but couldn't have the same dog, as the owner explained that since my last visit the DC dog had received Honours, and therefore did not go out on guide trips. I asked: "What does he do now then?"

"Oh, he just sits on his arse and barks!" was the reply.

•

On his way up to the Lodge last night, our Worshipful Master tripped over a gnome. The gnome immediately piped up, "Excuse me sir, but you look like a good-hearted soul. I've got my foot trapped and if you will release me, I will grant you one wish."

Our WM, always quick off the mark, swiftly released the gnome's foot and said, "Any wish? Well, as luck (and the joke) would have it, I ran over my wife's cat this morning and killed it outright. Do you think you could restore it to life for me?"

The gnome sat down heavily and said, "Ah, well, that's the problem you see. Much as I'd like to oblige, death is pretty terminal, and the G.A.O.T.U. takes a dim view of any of his subjects who think they know better. Can you not think of anything else?"

Our WM gave this some thought and finally said, "Well, I'm on my way to a Lodge meeting. Do you think you could just arrange it so that the Director of Ceremonies lets me get on with the degree without interfering, and the Past Masters sit silently behind me; and if I pause for breath, no-one tells me what I already know I should say next?"

And the gnome says, "Hmmmm. Let's take another look at that cat. . ."

•

## LONDON (EAST) RITUAL      OPENING THE LODGE

|  |  |
|---|---|
| WM: | OK Bruvvers, 'ere's the brief. |
| WM: | Tickle them ivories, John. |
| WM: | Bruvvers, 'elp us to open this 'ere gaff. |
| WM: | Bruvver. . .why do we 'ave to look lively? |
| JW: | To make sure the wood's in the 'ole, Guvnor. |
| WM: | Well, don't just stand there. |
| JW to IG: | OK, Bruvver. . . you 'eard the Guv |
| IG to JW: | Done, John. |
| JW to WM: | Done, Guv. |
| WM to SW: | The next bit? |
| SW: | To see that the Bruvvers are all in the firm. |
| WM: | Come on, Bruvvers, shake a leg. |
| WM to JW: | 'Ow much top brass in this 'ere drum? |
| JW: | Free Guv. You and the two oppo's wiv the cuffs. |
| WM to SW: | Bruvver SW, 'ow many others? |

| | |
|---|---|
| SW: | Free John, besides the bouncer, namely the bloke on the door and the two geezers wiv the pool cues. |
| WM to JW: | Where's the bouncer then? |
| JW: | Outside the gaff, all tooled up. |
| WM: | Why's that then? |
| JW: | 'E's packing a blade in case we're busted, Guv. |
| WM to SW: | The bloke on the door? |
| SW: | 'Overin abaht a bit. |
| WM: | Wot the 'ell for? |
| SW: | To check the tickets, admit new punters and do wot 'e's told by my oppo. |
| WM to JW: | Where's the JD? |
| JW: | Over there. |
| WM: | Why? |
| JW: | To grass to you, Guv, and chivvy 'em all up a bit. |
| WM to SW | And the other one? |
| SW: | Next to you, Guv. |
| WM: | Why? |
| SW: | Errand boy, Guvnor. |
| WM to JW: | Bruvver JW, wot abaht you? |
| JW: | On the sidelines, Guv. |
| WM: | Why? |
| JW: | To nip dahn the pub wiv the bruvvers, get some booze and grub, and get em all back 'ere before the last bell. |
| WM to SW: | Bruvver SW, wot abaht you? |
| SW: | Down the shallow end, Guv. |
| WM: | Wot the 'ell for? |
| SW: | To let 'em know when it's ligh'ing up time and to close down the gaff when all the bruvvers 'ave 'ad their cut. |
| WM to IPM: | Where am I? |
| IPM: | At the sharp end, Guv. |
| WM: | Why's that then? |
| IPM: | To keep them lot on their toes, open the gaff and get 'em at it. |
| WM: | Bruvvers, now that we're all 'ere, it's eyes down for a full 'ouse, but before we do, let's get the boss in the technical drawing department to tip us the wink so there's no aggro. |
| All: | Nice one, Guvnor! |

●

A team of archaeologists were excavating in Israel when they came upon a cave. Written across the wall of the cave were some curious symbols. It was considered a unique find and the writings were said to be at least three thousand years old! The piece of stone was removed, brought to the museum, and archaeologists from around the world came to study the ancient symbols.

They held a huge meeting after months of conferences to discuss the meaning of the markings. The President of the society pointed at the first drawing and said: 'This looks like a woman. We can judge that it was family oriented and held women in high esteem. You can also tell they were intelligent, as the next symbol resembles a donkey, so they were smart enough to have animals till the soil. The next drawing looks like a shovel of some sort, which means they even had tools to help them. Even further proof of their high intelligence is the fish, which means that if a famine had hit the earth, whereby the crops didn't grow, they would take to the sea for food. The last symbol appears to be the Star of David which means they were evidently Hebrews."

The audience applauded enthusiastically, but a little old man stood up at the back of the room and said: "Idiots, Hebrew is read from right to left. It says: 'Holy Mackerel, Dig the Ass on that Woman!'"

•

A wife heard her husband come back into the house not too long after he had left for the night.

She said: "Honey, I thought you were going to your Lodge meeting."

"It was postponed," he replied.

"The wife of the Generalissimo Grand Exalted Invincible Supreme Potentate wouldn't let him attend tonight."

•

I was asked, at the last minute, to reply on behalf of the guests. After the usual polite niceties, I then informed the assembled Brethren that the six men on the top table were my biological brothers. The first was an accountant and the second knew nothing about figures either, the third was a copper and the fourth occupied the cell next to him, the fifth was a financial advisor, and the sixth was also a rogue, and me, the seventh, well I am a bachelor, just like our father.

•

There once was an American who decided to write a book about famous Masonic Lodges around the world. For his first chapter he decided to write about English Lodges. So he booked his tickets and finally arrived in Liverpool, thinking that he would work his way across the country from west to east.

On his first day he was inside a Lodge taking photographs, when he noticed a golden telephone mounted on the wall with a sign that read '£10,000 per call'. The American, being intrigued, asked a Brother who was strolling by what the telephone was used for. The Brother replied that it was a direct line to Heaven and that for £10,000 you could talk to the Great Architect. The American thanked the Brother and went on his way.

The American's next stop was in Manchester. There, while at a very large Masonic Centre, he saw the same golden telephone with the same sign under it. He wondered if this was the same kind of telephone he saw in Liverpool and he asked a nearby Brother what its purpose was. The Brother told him that it was a direct line to Heaven and that for £10,000 he could talk to the Great Architect. "OK, thank you," said the American.

The American travelled on to Leeds, Birmingham, Leicester and many other places. At every Lodge he stopped at he saw the same golden telephone with the same '£10,000 per call' sign under it, and every time the American asked a member of the Lodge what the phone was for he got the same answer — "It's a direct line to Heaven and for £10,000 you can talk to the Great Architect."

Finally, the American arrived at Great Queen Street and again he saw the same golden telephone but this time the sign under it read '10p per call'. The American was intrigued and he told a Grand Officer: "Most Worshipful Brother, I have travelled all over England and I have seen this same golden telephone in many Lodges. I have found out that it is a direct line to Heaven, but in all the other cities the cost to call Heaven was £10,000. Why is it so cheap here?"

The Most Worshipful Brother smiled and answered: "You are in London now, son. It's a local call."

•

While acting as IG, I asked our candidate if he felt anything. Being a true Scotsman, he replied: "A wee prick."

Our JD, realising his mistake, leaned over and whispered: "I do."

Later, at festive board, I rose to congratulate him but also stated I had a concern about his hearing. "When I greeted you at the door of the Lodge I asked you if you felt anything . . . not who you were with!"

•

Worshipful Master: "Brother Senior Warden, the labours of the evening being ended, you have my command to close the Lodge."

Senior Warden: "Worshipful Master, Brethren, in the name of . . . (mumbles and looks confused) . . . Good God! What's his name again . . ?"

•

Most Masons are very law-abiding but some of them get mixed up when it comes to the difference between the amount of alcohol you can take through Customs and the amount you are allowed to drink and drive.

•

I was talking to Martin and Josh about joining their Lodge. Josh said there were two types of member:
"I'm a Full Member, and Martin's a Country Member."
"Yes," I said. "I remember, but you speak that way of your Brothers?"

•

A young Entered Apprentice was being tested on his memory and proficiency. After displaying the signs and passwords he had learned, he asked: "I have noticed several of the older members sticking their fingers in their ears and whistling. What does that sign mean?"
"That's not a sign," replied the DC. "That's just the Past Masters adjusting their hearing aids."

•

Knock! Knock! Knock!
"Who's there?"
Knock! Knock! Knock!
"Who's there?!"
"Hang on! Don't you mean — whom have you there?"

•

**Masonic Survival Kit**

Always make sure that the following items are in your regalia case whenever you attend a meeting:
Why these items?

Toothpick
Rubber Band
A Plaster
Pencil

Eraser
Chewing Gum
Mint
Tea Bag

### 1. TOOTHPICK
To remind you to pick out the good qualities in others. *Matt. 7:1*

### 2. RUBBER BAND
To remind you to be flexible; things might not always go the way you want, but it will work out. *Romans 8:28*

### 3. A PLASTER
To remind you to heal hurt feelings, yours or someone else's. *Col. 3:12-14*

### 4. PENCIL
To remind you to list your blessings every day. *Eph. 1:3*

### 5. ERASER
To remind you that everyone makes mistakes, and it's OK. *Gen. 50:15-21*

### 6. CHEWING GUM
To remind you to stick with it and you can accomplish anything. *Phil. 4:13*

### 7. MINT
To remind you that you are worth a mint! *John 3:16-17*

### 8. TEA BAG
To remind you to relax daily and go over that list of blessings. *1 Thess. 5:18*

•

A tired old Mason
whose hair was grey,
Came to the gates
of Heaven one day.
When asked what, on Earth,
he had done the most,
He said he had replied to the
Visitor's Toast.
St Peter said,
as he tolled the bell,
"Come inside my Brother,
you've had enough of Hell."

•

I always thought a Freemason was a man who builds houses for nothing.

•

I was once a visitor at a Lodge and was introduced to the Tate family.
First there was the old man WM DIC-TATE, who wants to run everything his way, and his cousin WBro RO-TATE who wants to change everything.
Brother AGI-TATE stirs up trouble with his nephew Bro IRRI-TATE.
When new ideas are suggested Bro HESI-TATE and his son VEGE-TATE both want to leave them until next year.
Brother IMI-TATE wants everything to be like it was in his Mother Lodge.
Brother DEVAS-TATE is a voice of doom — but Brother FACILI-TATE is most helpful.
Brother COGI-TATE and Brother MEDI-TATE think things over carefully — but poor old Brother AMPU-TATE has cut himself off completely.

•

Fred was eager to progress and never turned down a request, even at short notice.
   Some started to take advantage of him until one morning he was having a lie-in when the telephone went at 7:30am. Before he could speak, he was asked to attend a 10am meeting, nearly two hours' drive away. He passed it to his wife, saying, loudly enough to be heard on the phone:
   "Darling! I think someone wants your husband."

A candidate for initiation in a country Lodge had been teased at length about what was going to happen to him.

Unfortunately, one Brother attending came straight from market where he had bought a goat, which was tethered outside.

The candidate arrived, saw the goat and fled, never to be seen again.

Have you heard the story about that Mason who wanted to go hunting? He
needed a dog and consulted a Brother. That Brother, who sold dogs, gave him one,
called JW.

"It's a very good dog," he said. "He knows a lot about hunting and you can
truly rely on him."

Our fellow took that dog. One week later, he returned. "It's not too bad, but he
doesn't seem to be very experienced. Haven't you got another dog?"

"Sure I have," said the Brother. "This one, for example, is called SW and he's a
bit more experienced. Try him and if you don"t like him, feel free to come back."

Indeed, our fellow returned the dog two weeks later. "He's quite good actually,
but he's not what I'm looking for. Still I need a dog which is more experienced."

"Well," said the Brother, "I can offer you a really experienced dog. He's called
PM and you'll have good time with him."

So, our fellow took the animal. Just one day later, he returned.

"What's wrong with him?" the Brother asked. "I haven't got another dog that is
more experienced than this one."

"Well," our fellow said, "he might be experienced, but all he's doing is sitting
there and barking!"

•

The Grand Master, Grand Secretary and Grand Treasurer are walking to lunch
when they find an antique oil lamp. They rub it and a Genie comes out in a puff
of smoke.

The Genie says: "I usually grant only three wishes, so I'll give each of you just
one."

"Me first! Me first!" says Grand Treasurer.
"I want to be in the Bahamas, driving a speedboat, without a care in the world."
Poof! He's gone.

"Me next! Me next!" says Grand Secretary in astonishment. "I want to be in
Hawaii, relaxing on the beach with my personal masseuse, an endless supply of
pina coladas and the love of my life." Poof! He's gone.

"OK, you're up," the Genie says to the Grand Master.
The Grand Master says: "I want those two back in the office after lunch."
Moral of this story:
Always let your Grand Master have the first say.

•

Once upon a time there was a Lodge located in the backwoods of rural England, where the Brethren were all faithful Masons but lacked the knowledge of receiving Brothers from other jurisdictions. During one of the meetings the Junior Deacon informs the Worshipful Master that there is an alarm at the door, whereupon the WM replies: "Attend the alarm and report your findings." The Junior Deacon opens the door and sees to his amazement a Brother impeccably dressed with an elaborate apron and jewels about his chest.

The Tyler being somewhat slow to answer for the visiting Brother, the visitor states: "My name is John Smith, PM of my Lodge, Past District Deputy Grand Master of my district, Past Grand Master of My Grand Lodge, who humbly requests an audience with the Worshipful Master."

The Junior Deacon, upon hearing those words from the visitor and seeing the elaborate apron and jewels upon his chest, immediately closes the door, returns to his post and informs the Worshipful Master: "Worshipful Master, The Grand Architect of the Universe is at the door!"

●

They say Freemasonry is universal but...

...If an Ephraimite applied to join, would he be able to progress beyond the First Degree?

●

One doddery old Secretary, well past his sell-by date, delivers the Second Degree tracing board to the Lodge.

Though his effort is admirable, the performance is really very slow.

The Brethren all have respect for him due to his age and his Grand Rank, but really what should have been completed in 20 minutes takes almost double that time.

Once the presentation is over the Master speaks, thanking him for his effort on behalf of the Lodge, and asks him to write letters of condolence to the families of the forty and two thousand Ephraimites reported slain during the presentation!

●

One poor Mason whose mind was on the festive board ended the meeting with: "All that is left is for us to lock up our secrets in the sacred suppository."

The Brethren of the Lodge united in the act of laughing loud in response to this one!

●

During the car journey home from a Masonic meeting on a dark stormy night, a Mason loses it on a corner, ending up quite safe but stuck in a ditch. He staggers up to the road and the first set of headlights that come along are those of a tractor driven by a farmer. He stops and willingly tows him out of the ditch and insists he follow him to his farm just down the road, where he is offered overnight accommodation, the use of the telephone and a bath. In the morning his clothes have been cleaned and pressed and a hearty breakfast is provided. In thanking the farmer they shake hands and the Mason realises that the farmer is a Brother. "Well, there you go," he says, "I suppose you did all that because you realised I was on the Square by my black tie and Masonic bag in the car etc." The farmer smiles and replies: "No my friend, I did it not because you are a Mason but rather that I am!"

•

Did you hear the one about the poor candidate for initiation who had diarrhoea?
　　He didn't know whether to roll his trouser leg up, or pull his pants down!

•

The first Lodge meeting under the auspices of the newly appointed Worshipful Master was off to a good start, and the Secretary was reading the minutes of the last meeting – the installation ceremony. At one stage he paused, and said to the WM, "There were 27 Past Masters and 43 members in attendance. Will you take their names as read Worshipful Master?"
　　"No," said the WM. "If you wouldn't mind, I would like to hear their names."
　　The disgruntled Secretary duly obliged and paused to say, "I received 17 apologies Worshipful Master; will you take their names as read?"
　　"I would much rather hear their names, Worshipful Brother Secretary," said the WM. The Secretary read out the names, but the tone of his voice did little to disguise his feelings. The ceremony that evening was the Second Degree, and the Secretary was delivering the explanation of the tracing board. When he reached the part 'and there fell on that day forty and two thousand Ephraimites,' he turned to the WM and said, "Will you take their names as read, Worshipful Master?"

•

Q:　　How many Masons does it take to change a light bulb?
A:　　Change it? Never! My grandfather donated that bulb to the Lodge!

•

A Brother had committed murder, and on arrival at the gallows he remonstrated with the hangman, declaring, "You cannot go through with this execution! I'm a Mason!"

The hangman replied, "I don't know anything about that. Step off with your left foot."

•

A newly installed WM was determined to pack as much as possible into his year of office and to that end he visited Brother George, who had recently taken up residence in a nursing home. During the drive to the nursing home, the WM revelled in the thought that George would be very impressed to have a visit from his WM. Ten minutes into his visit, the WM began to doubt if George had recognised him so he asked, "George, do you know who I am?"

"No," said George. "But if you ask the matron, she will tell you who you are."

•

A nervous Brother was performing the First Degree Charge. As his nerves got the better of him, his actions became faster and faster. To make matters worse, as he fidgeted in his chair, he knocked his gavel off the pedestal. One wise Past Master remarked to another, "Did you hear the Masonic boom?"

•

The ceremony had reached the point when every officer had been appointed with the exception of the Tyler. The Director of Ceremonies took up his position in front of the newly appointed WM, stood to order and froze. The DC and the WM looked at each other without a word being spoken. Eventually, the silence was broken when a well-intentioned prompter shouted in a broad cockney accent, "Who's yah Tylah?" In reply, a Brother said, "Montague Burton."

•

A senior member of a Lodge was well known for organising fraternal visits: between two and five visits per year. However, one such trip that made the others look very ordinary was the fraternal visit to one of the oldest Lodges in the USA. Such was the interest of the members of his Lodge, plus those from other Lodges, he was able to fill every seat on the plane.

With their visit over, they all gathered in the departure lounge waiting for their flight home. It was then the pilot sought out the Brother organiser with the news that the flight home would be unique as every member of the crew was a Mason. A buzz of excitement spread through the assembled Masons, which was heightened when someone suggested that the flight could be even more unique if they carried out a ceremony 40,000 feet above the Atlantic. Everyone thought the suggestion was an excellent one except the Lodge Secretary, who felt they should have higher authority, such as permission from the Provincial Grand Master.

The dauntless Brother organiser dashed to the nearest telephone to ring the PGM. forgetting that the time in the UK would be different to that in the States. In fact, it was 3.40am when the PGM was called to the phone and, as he hadn't got to bed until gone one o'clock, he wasn't best pleased. However, he listened attentively and said that it would be fine for them to hold a ceremony on board the plane, but politely pointed out that they could have done so without asking him. Before putting down the phone, he said to the Brother organiser, "When the officers are being appointed, it would be my pleasure to appoint you as Tyler."

•

"The festive board is going well," said one Brother to the JW. "Shall we let them have fun a little more or would you like to do your toast for the visitors now?"

•

A man new to Masonry was talking with his friend and said, "We have Grand Officers in our Lodge who are very religious."

"How come?" said his friend.

"Well, every time our new master does the Ritual, they put their heads in their hands and say, 'Oh my God!' "

•

I am a Staffordshire Mason, but my commitment to Masonry was cemented when I realised the depths of support that Brothers provide to one another. One bad winter, I visited the Baldock Lodge of Harmony in Hertfordshire. The ceremony was enthralling and it was with great amazement that I left the Festive Board to discover five inches of snow had fallen whilst we were in the Lodge. I stood at the top of the steps and said to myself, "I don't fancy driving 110 miles in that."

"Then don't," said a voice at my elbow. It came from one of the visitors who lived nearby. He invited me into his home to sit by a roaring log fire, enjoy a welcome nightcap and a good night's sleep. I met his wife and in no time was deep in conversation about Masonry and its attributes. It was only when I got home the next morning that I realised I hadn't phoned my wife to explain where I was. She was furious and demanded to know who had so graciously put me up. I told her I didn't really know, except that it was one of the Masters from a Hertfordshire Lodge. I went to work in deep trouble, but when I got home I found that my enterprising wife had obtained a list of every Master of every Lodge in Hertfordshire.

"Did one of them confirm my story?" I asked.

"Oh yes," she said. "They all did."

•

A man told his wife that he wasn't feeling too well. She suggested that he should make an appointment to see his doctor. The GP examined him but said he could not find the cause of the problem. He was then advised to go and see a specialist at the local hospital. A specialist examined him and said he had some bad news. He was informed that he had a very rare disease called Yellow 41 and had only six months to live.

When he arrived home, he was totally devastated. After explaining the situation to his wife she pointed out that, as his days were numbered, if there was anything he wanted to do, this was the time to do it. He gave the matter some thought and eventually admitted that he had always wanted to play bingo but could never find the time.

"We will go tonight," said his wife. So that evening they made their way to the local bingo hall. Much to everyone's surprise, he won every game throughout the entire evening. At the end of the session he approached the MC to collect his winnings.

The MC said, "I have run this organisation for many years and I have never come across anyone who has won everything right through the whole evening. You are a very lucky man."

"Lucky man?" came the reply. "I've got Yellow 41."

"I don't believe it," said the MC. "You have even won the raffle!"

•

The working tool of a Past Master: In an orchestra, the triangle is a minor percussion instrument. It is used infrequently and has little significance in the overall texture of the music but adds brilliance and emphasis in the quieter passages of a performance. But as we are not all musical or melodic Masons, we must apply this tool to ourselves. Masonically, it teaches us that having vacated the Chair of King Solomon and contemplated the difficulties which accompany that great responsibility, having boldly perfected our Ritual and in spite of all distractions and advice delivered, we are reminded, as Past Masters, to sit quietly in the East and observe the proceedings of the Lodge, to contribute little and chime in only at moments of particular gravity with telling sage comments (or the occasional 'wrong' prompt).

•

Q:    A Lodge of Masons wants to change a bulb and have only a small table to stand on. How long will it take to change the bulb?

A:    They'll never do it. They'll be too busy helping each other get on the table!

•

If you have a problem remembering Ritual, spare a thought for this couple. While on a road trip, an elderly couple had lunch at a roadside restaurant. After finishing their meal, they left the restaurant to resume their trip. The elderly woman unknowingly left her glasses on the table and didn't miss them until they had been driving for twenty minutes and, to add to their aggravation, they had to travel quite a distance before they could find the opportunity to turn around and return to the restaurant.

On the return journey, the husband turned into the clichéd grouchy old man. He fussed, complained and scolded his wife relentlessly. The more he chided her, the more agitated he became- he wouldn't let up for one minute. To her relief, they finally arrived at the restaurant. As the woman got out of the car and hurried inside to retrieve her glasses, the old geezer yelled, "While you're in there, you might as well get my hat and the credit card!"

•

One of our Brethren was telling me that he has just returned from Australia where he visited an outback Lodge. At the Festive Board, he noticed pieces of meat hanging from the ceiling. Curiosity got the better of him and he asked the Brother sitting next to him what the decorations were doing there.

"Ah," said the Brother. "One of our Brothers, who has now passed on, left us a legacy that provided meat for our barbie with the proviso that the Brother requiring a free meal only had to jump up and pull meat off the string. However, if he failed to do so, he had to buy drinks all round."

"Oh," I said. "Did you have a go?"

"No," he replied. "The steaks were too high."

•

This is especially for members of the Royal Ark Mariner Lodges. In the year 2008, the Lord came unto Noah, who was now living in England, and said, "Once again the Earth has become wicked and overpopulated, and I see the end of all flesh before me. Build another ark and save two of every living thing along with a few good humans."

He gave Noah the drawings saying, "You have six months to build the ark before I start the unending rain for forty days and forty nights." Six months later, the Lord looked down and saw Noah weeping in his yard but with no ark in sight. "Noah!" he roared. "I'm about to start the rain. Where is the ark?"

"Forgive me, Lord," begged Noah, "but things have changed. I needed building regulations approval and I've been arguing with the fire brigade about the need for a sprinkler system. My neighbours claim that I should have obtained planning permission for building the ark in my garden because it is a development of the site, even though in my view it is a temporary structure.

"We then had to appeal to the Secretary of State for a decision. The Department of Transport demanded a bond be posted for the future costs of moving power lines and overhead obstructions to clear the passage of the ark's move to the sea. I told them that the sea would be coming to us, but they would hear nothing of it. Getting the wood was another problem. All the decent trees have preservation orders on them and we live in a 'site of special scientific interest' set up in order to protect the Little Owl. I tried to convince the environmentalists that I needed the wood to save the owls, but again no-go. When I started gathering the animals the RSPCA sued me. They insisted that I was confining wild animals against their will. They argued the accommodation was too restrictive and it was cruel and inhumane to put so many animals in a confined space.

"Then the County Council, the Environment Agency and the Rivers Authority ruled that I couldn't build the ark until they'd conducted an environmental impact study on your proposed flood. I'm still trying to resolve a complaint with the Equal Opportunities Commission on how many disabled carpenters I'm supposed to hire for my building team. The trades unions say I can't use my sons. They insist I have to hire only accredited workers with ark-building experience. The health and safety people insist on having one of their inspectors on site twenty-four hours a day at my expense. To make matters worse, Customs and Excise seized all my assets, claiming I'm trying to leave the country illegally with endangered species. So forgive me Lord, but it would take at least ten years for me to finish this ark."

Suddenly the skies cleared, the sun began to shine and a rainbow stretched across the sky. Noah looked up in wonder and asked, "You mean you're not going to destroy the world?"

"No," said the Lord. "The British Government beat me to it!"

It has been reported in our Lodge that a motorcar was spotted travelling on the M25 at a very slow speed. A motorway patrol was alerted, found the car and pulled it over. On enquiry, a policeman found that an old Provincial Officer was driving his Provincial Master to a meeting. The policeman asked why the driver was proceeding so slowly, and he replied that it was the M25.

"Yes, it is. But why so slowly?" asked the policeman. After further questioning, it dawned on him that the driver was convinced that, as it was the M25, he was restricted to 25mph. At this point, groans and whimpers were heard coming from the back of the car. Shining a torch into the back seat, the policeman discovered the Provincial Master curled into a foetal position, with his head in his hands and a look of terror on his face.

"My God!" cried the copper. "What on earth is wrong with him?"

"I don't know," the Provincial Officer replied. "He's been like that since we turned off the B182."

•

Q:    What kind of car did King Solomon's father drive?
A:    According to Scripture, the roar of David's Triumph was heard throughout the land.

•

Did you hear about the dairy farmer who became a Mason?
He kept giving everyone the secret milkshake.

•

Two men out driving passed a Masonic Lodge. One said to the other, "I have always wondered what that building was."

"I'm sure it's a betting shop," said his friend.

"I'm sure you're wrong," he replied.

"Anyway, what makes you think that?"

"Well, as I was walking past the other day, I saw two gentlemen talking and I overheard one of them saying, 'So far I have had a first, two seconds and one third.'"

•

A Mason went to a friend's house to practise his Ritual and listened to his friend initiate his parrot. He was amazed that the parrot could repeat the whole First Degree Ritual and asked as if the bird knew the Second Degree Ritual. "No," said his friend. "He is rubbish and falls off the perch when he does the signs."

•

Q:      How many Past Masters does it take to change a light bulb?
A:      None. That's the Secretary's job.

•

A doctor was examining one of his patients who was very nervous. The doctor realised that he was a fellow Mason and, to put him at his ease when the examination was over, he said: "You may now retire in order to restore yourself to your own personal comforts."

To which the patient replied, "Yes, and on my return you will no doubt render the usual charge!"

•

A man is drifting in a hot air balloon when the clouds become dense and navigation becomes impossible. He lets air escape from the balloon and descends through the clouds where he can see a man riding a bicycle. The balloonist calls down, "Where am I?"

The cyclist looks up and shouts, "You are in a balloon."

"You must be the local Lodge IPM," replied the balloonist.

"Why, yes I am! But how on earth did you know that?" replied the startled cyclist.

"Well, your information is one hundred per cent accurate and one hundred per cent useless!"

•

Three men are debating who has the greatest claim to the oldest professional: a surgeon, a solicitor and the WM. The surgeon said that as God created woman from the rib of man, it was obviously the work of a surgeon.

"Nonsense!" replied the solicitor. "It says in the Bible that God created order out of chaos, which was obviously the work of a legal mind such as mine."

"Sorry, gentlemen," the WM concluded. "We are the oldest. After all, who do you think created the chaos in the first place?"

•

The Pope and the WM are debating who has the greatest powers. So the challenge is laid down – whoever can walk on water will be judged the greatest. The Pope starts first and is soon up to his neck in water and gives in. The WM walks across the lake with only the soles of his shoes touching the water.

"I have to concede," the Pope said.

As they walk away, the SW says to the WM, "Should we tell him where the stepping stones are?"

•

Our WM claims to be a good golfer but when he tried to drown himself, he failed because he couldn't keep his head down long enough.

•

The medical definition of 'brain death' is the man who enjoys the JW's jokes about the visitors!

•

If wind surfers do it standing up and rugby players do it with odd shaped balls, Freemasons do it craftily.

•

Q: What do Hiram Abiff, George Washington and a tombstone cutter have in common?
A: They're all monumental masons.

•

Three Past Masters were discussing what epitaphs they wanted carved on their tombstones when they died. The first said, "I want it to state that I served my Lodge well, put our finances in order and resolved all problems. It should also mention that it was I who implemented many of our social programmes."

The second said, "I want them to say that I raised more new Brothers than any Past Master we ever had. I raised the standard of our Ritual in the Lodge. They should say that I instituted community programmes and brought true Masonic ideals to our non-Masonic neighbours." They both looked to the third Past Master and asked him what words he would like on his tombstone.

He said, "Look, he's moving!"

•

## Lodge Humour
The Structure of the Lodge

The Right Worshipful Master,
Leaps tall buildings in a single bound,
Is more powerful than an express train,
Is faster than a speeding bullet,
Walks on water and gives policy to God.

The Worshipful Senior Warden,
Leaps short buildings with a single bound,
Is more powerful than a goods train,
Is just as fast as a speeding bullet,
Walks on the water if the sea is calm and talks with God.

The Worshipful Junior Warden,
Leaps short buildings with a running start and a favourable wind,
Is almost as powerful as a goods train,
Is faster than a speeding air gun pellet,
Walks on water of a paddling pool and talks with
God if special dispensation is given.

The Senior Deacon,
Barely clears a garden hut,
Loses a tug-of-war with a train,
Can fire a speeding bullet,
Swims well and is occasionally addressed by God.

The Junior Deacon,
Makes splat marks on the wall when trying to leap buildings,
Is run over by trains,
Can sometimes handle a gun without inflicting self-injury,
Doggie paddles and talks with the animals.

The Inner Guard,
Runs headlong into buildings,
Recognises trains two out of three times, Is not issued ammunition,
Can stay afloat with a life jacket and talks to walls.

The Steward,
Falls over doorsteps when trying to enter buildings,
Says, "Look at the choo choos",
Wets himself with a water pistol,
Plays in mud puddles and mumbles to himself.

The Secretary,
Lifts buildings and walks under them,
Kicks trains off the tracks,
Catches speeding bullets in his mouth and eats them,
Freezes water with a single glance.
He is God!

•

Visiting our Lodge in a rural backwater of Aberdeen, a Brother from London was talking to the Secretary about the well-known and important men that belonged to his fine London Lodge. "So, have any big men been born around here?" he asked the Secretary.

"No, the best we can do are babies. Different in London I suppose?"

•

The RWM was in hospital recovering from an operation and the Secretary visited to update him on the meeting he had missed. "Your apologies were duly noted and I informed the Brethren assembled the reason you were unable to attend. The WSW proposed and the WJW seconded that you be wished a speedy recovery. The proposal was duly put to the Brethren and the result was 22 for, 18 against and 7 abstentions."

•

The MWGMM was planning a Grand Lodge trip to visit the Grand Lodge of Hawaii. He asked the Grand Secretary to investigate the protocols and made a special request that he find out the local pronunciation of Hawaii. Was it 'Ha-wai-ee' or 'Ha-vai-ee'? The Grand Secretary duly called his counterpart in Hawaii and, after discussing the nature of the planned visit, asked the question. "Ha-vai-ee," replied the voice on the phone.

"Great! Thanks for your help," the Grand Secretary replied.
"You're velcome."

•

A Mason was telling one of his fellows about the trouble he was having with his Ritual. His friend said he knew a Brother who sold parrots that know the Ritual and prompt you when you have any trouble. So the next day he went to the shop. After strict examination, the owner pulled a curtain to reveal three parrots. The first was wearing a RWM's apron, the second a DoC's apron and the third a PM's apron.

"How much is the one with the RWM's apron?"

"£6,000. He knows all the Ritual, including the inner workings, and will always prompt you when you get stuck," the owner said.

"No, too expensive. What about the one with the DoC's apron?"

"Well, that one is only £2,000. He doesn't know the inner workings, but knows most of the Ritual and will always prompt you when learning," replied the owner.

"No, still too much, I'm afraid. What about the one wearing the PM's apron?"

"Oh, I can let you have him for just £10!" the owner suggested.

"Why so cheap? He must know all the Ritual and the inner workings."

"Oh yes," said the owner. "He knows all the Ritual, but when you make a mistake all he does is mutter 'Tut, tut, tut'!"

•

Two candidates were elected to enter on the same Lodge night; one was a butcher and the other a sales rep. On the night of initiation the butcher went in first but when it came to the charge at the North East corner it was discovered that he had a quarter pound of liver in his pocket that he was due to deliver on his way home; obviously this had to be taken away. So the JD took this to the Tyler and said, "This is the butcher's liver, please keep it safe." Funnily enough, to this day we haven't seen the sales rep again!

•

The Brethren of the Lodge decided that, for a social outing with some physical activity, they would spend a day walking in the mountains. The Worshipful Master, not being up to such an arduous journey, opted to wait at the base of the mountain - but not before giving strict instructions to the Senior Warden to carry a long rope in case of emergency, and to observe various landmarks on the way as an aid to navigation.

Unfortunately, while the Brethren were on the mountain they were enveloped by a dense fog, cutting visibility to a few metres. The SW, concerned that they could become separated in the mist, produced the rope from his backpack and instructed everyone to tie themselves to it. Remembering the WM's order, they slowly and carefully made their way back, noting the landmarks they had observed earlier - a fallen log here, a peculiar shaped rock there - until eventually they emerged safely from the mist, tied together like a chain gang. The WM was overjoyed to greet them. "I was very worried when the mist covered the mountain," he said. "How did you find your way back without anyone getting lost?"

"Isn't it obvious?" replied the SW. "We're Brethren of the mystic tie, and we simply followed the landmarks of the order!"

•

A candidate was sitting with his proposer and seconder at Harmony after his initiation. "Who was that sitting on the WM's left?" he asked.

"That was the IPM," his proposer replied.

"And on his right?" asked the candidate.

"That was the Provincial Grand Master."

"I see," said the candidate. "So why did the WM keep interrupting them while they were doing the degree?"

•

A ninety-five-year-old Past Master got married to a lovely bride of eighteen. As they climbed into bed on their wedding night, he asked, "Did your mother teach you the facts of life?" His new wife blushed and shyly shook her head.

"That's a pity. I've forgotten what they are."

A new EA was chatting to some of his Brethren in the Harmony after the meeting. "I think I've got most of the signs, but what's the meaning of the one where you put your finger in your ear and whistle?"
His proposer replied, "It means that the Past Masters' hearing aids are turned up too high again!"

Q:    How many Cowans does it take to change a light bulb?
A:    None. They are in eternal darkness.

•

One day a Brother discovers a small village somewhere in the north east of Scotland. He is curious to know if there is a Masonic Lodge, so he takes a walk through the village and after some time he finds a path called Mason's Road. Thinking that the path might lead to the Masonic Temple, he follows it. At the end of the pathway he sees a building, which appears somewhat rotten and out of use for quite a while. Our Brother tries to open the door and, surprisingly, it's not locked. He goes inside and finds dust and spider webs everywhere. In front of a particular door sits a skeleton wearing an apron and collar, holding a sword in its bony hand.

"Oh my goodness!" says our Brother in surprise as he enters the Lodge room. In puzzlement, he sees skeletons adorned in collars and aprons throughout the room: the RWM, Wardens, Organist and Deacons – all skeletons. He looks around the room and studies the seats of the Secretary and Treasurer. Under the hand of the Treasurer, he finds a small piece of paper, a note possibly intended to have been passed to the Secretary. So our Brother picks up the note, blows away the dust and reads, "If nobody prompts the WM soon, we'll be sitting here forever!"

•

The WM and his two Wardens went golfing one day. As they were about to tee off the first hole, the course marshal asked if a young woman could join them. Being a charitable group they all agreed. She turned out to be a scratch golfer, but on the eighteenth hole she drove the green in two and was about to putt for an eagle. She then told the three Brothers that if any one of them helped her make the putt she would be eternally grateful. The Junior Warden looked at the putt and told her it was uphill and broke to the right. The Senior Warden, being a more expert workman, looked at it and said, "That is partially correct but five inches from the hole, it breaks to the left."

The WM then took his turn. He looked at the putt and the young lady very carefully, then went over to the ball, picked it up and exclaimed, "It's a gimme!"

•

Q:	How many Past Masters does it take to change a light bulb?
A:	One. However, it will take him a year to find an authentic antique Edison bulb in keeping with the ancient landmarks.

•

One day an English Mason, a Scottish Mason, and an Irish Mason were in the bar after the meeting.
They each proceeded to buy a pint of Guinness.
Just as they were about to enjoy their creamy beverage, a fly landed in each of their pints and became stuck in the thick head.
The Englishman pushed his beer from him in disgust.
The Irishman fished the offending fly out of his beer and continued drinking it as if nothing had happened.
The Scotsman picked the fly out of his drink, held it out over the beer and yelled,
	"SPIT IT OOT!! SPIT IT OOT!!!!"

•

"OLD MASTER MASONS NEVER DIE,
BUT YOU'LL HAVE TO JOIN TO FIND OUT WHY"

•

I do not attend the meetings for I've not the time to spare,
But every time they have a feast you will surely find me there.
I cannot help with the degrees for I do not know the work,
But I can applaud the speakers and handle a knife and fork.
I'm so rusty in the Ritual, it seems like Greek to me,
But practice has made me perfect in the Knife and Fork Degree.

•

A travelling salesman is standing at a bar in a small village and starts to berate and criticise the Craft. He then asks the barman if he wants to hear a funny joke about the Masons. The barman reveals that he is a Mason, the other barman is a Mason, the people beside him are Masons, and the man entering the bar is also a Mason. "So do you still want to tell your joke?" asks the barman.
	"Not if I have to explain it five times over!" the salesman replies.

•

A doctor is about to carry out a physical on a Jewish patient. "I won't let anyone touch me who doesn't have kosher hands!" says the patient. Seeing the depth of his conviction, the doctor calls round the hospital to find a Jewish doctor to perform the examination. Finally, he finds one on the eighth floor, explains the predicament and asks if the Jewish doctor could assist.

"Sorry, I've got my own problems here," says his colleague. "I've got five Catholics who won't pee in a Mason jar."

•

A newly raised MM was going for a job interview and knew that his interviewer was a prominent member of the Craft. He took great care to wear his ring, lapel-badge, cufflinks, neck chain and other Masonic jewellery. The interview was going well, although he had not been given any indication of recognition. At the end of the interview, he was asked as to what salary package he was looking for and said, "Oh, £55,000 a year and six weeks' paid holiday."

The interviewer looked him straight in the eye and replied, "We'll halve it and you begin!"

•

Did you hear about the Lodge that was holding meetings in the function room of a local hotel while its temple was undergoing renovations? One evening, a travelling salesman asked the receptionist who the men in the function room were. The receptionist replied, "Oh, those are the Masons."

The salesman said, "I've always wanted to join the Masons. Do you think that they would let me in?"

"Oh no," the receptionist answered. "They're very exclusive. Why, you see that poor bloke standing outside the door with a sword in his hand? He's been knocking for six months and they still won't let him in!"

•

In the days of the Old West, a young fellow held up a bank, and in so doing shot and killed the teller. Several people witnessed his terrible crime and were able to identify him as he rode out of town. A posse was formed and the fugitive was captured and sent to jail back in the town. He was duly tried and sentenced to hang for his crime. On the appointed day of the execution, a scaffold was erected outside the jail. As the fellow was led up the stairs to the scaffold, the judge read his sentence and asked him if he had anything to say.

"I sure do, judge. If it wasn't for the Masons, I wouldn't be here." The judge enquired as to what he was referring. "Well, the sheriff who pursued me is a Mason, as was most of the posse. The jury was mostly Masons, and you, judge, are a Mason. If it wasn't for the Masons, I wouldn't be here."

That being all he had to say, the judge ordered the hangman to proceed. The hangman placed a hood over the fellow's head, put the rope around his neck, took him by the left arm and said, "You will now take one short step with your left foot."

Q: Why did the crocodile refuse to eat Freemasons?
A: Because they would lodge in its throat.

Q: What did the Junior Warden say when the Steward was about to serve double helpings at the Festive Board?
A: Halve it and begin.

The wife of a new Mason was constantly pestering her husband to tell her what happens at Lodge meetings. He finally gave in and said that they hire a stripper to dance naked. "Do you look?" she asked.

"Of course I look," he said, "Otherwise I'd be an Oddfellow."

Q:      What is the difference between a tyler and a tiler?
A:      One tyles lodges and the other lodges tiles.

•

## Gone before . . .

There was once a very senior and respected Mason who lived in the northernmost part of the north of England, and was the treasurer of a splendid lodge in northwest London.

The Brethren held their Ladies Festival in early summer, and on this particular year the temperature in southern England soared to 38 degrees centigrade (about 99 Fahrenheit).

The Worshipful Brother decided to precede his wife and spend a day working in the capital before she came down to join him for the event.
So he took the Great North Eastern Railway down to London and found his way to his hotel.

After he had settled into his room, he decided to send his wife a quick email. Unable to find the scrap of paper on which he had written her email address, he did his best to type it in from memory.

Unfortunately, he got one letter wrong and his note was directed instead to the elderly wife of a Bishop, whose husband had passed away only the day before. When the grieving widow checked her email, she took one look at the monitor, let out a terrible scream, clutched her chest and fell dead upon the floor.

At the sound, her family rushed into the room, found her lying there, and someone noticed this message on the screen:

*Dearest Wife,*

*Have just checked in. Everything prepared for your arrival tomorrow.*

*Your Loving Husband.*
*ps: Sure is hot down here!*

•

A well-known Brother once wanted to affiliate to a Lodge only a few miles away from his Mother Lodge. He went through the motions of obtaining a demit from his Mother Lodge and presenting it to the Secretary of his chosen Lodge, along with his application for affiliation. When asked what his reasons for wanting to move were, he replied, "Health reasons."

"That's a fairly unusual reason for wanting to move. If I'm not being too nosy, what's the problem?" asked the Secretary.

"They got sick of me over there!"

•

Some years back, just after the introduction of random breath testing, the police officers of a small country town had to show the community that the scheme against drink driving was having an effect. They decided to stake out the local Masonic Hall. As the night wore on, a Mason slowly came down the stairs, searched his pockets several times before finding his keys, and after having difficulties in locating the lock, eventually got in his car. The moment he started the engine, the two police officers approached and asked him to blow in the bag. He did as he was told, and, to the amazement of the officers, the test proved negative.

Fearing that the bag was faulty, the officers tried again but with the same results. Sure of a conviction, they escorted him to the police station for a blood test. However, it was negative. Upset with their lack of damning evidence, the officers asked him what he had done that evening. "Well, the Master was there, the Secretary was there, the Treasurer was there. In fact, all the office-bearers were there and we all had a great time," he answered.

"So, what's your office?" one of the policeman asked.

"Can't you guess?" says our man. "I was the Senior Decoy!"

•

In days of old, a Brother Knight had his squire polish his best armour, and had his groom prepare his best charger. On seeing this activity his fair lady said, "If you're going to that Lodge again, you'd better be back before 10.30pm or I'm raising the drawbridge and you're out for the night."

"Yes, dear," he replied as he packed his apron into his saddlebag and headed off to the meeting. At 10.13pm, there had been a bit of Harmony at the close of the meeting. With alarm, Sir Knight looked at his moondial and noticed the time. He downed the last of his mead, grabbed his apron, leapt to his charger and set off at full gallop towards the castle. 10.20pm and he was on the home straight. However, though the castle was in view the horse was tiring. In desperation, the knight spurred his steed for the final run as time ran out. 10.29pm and with only yards to go, the drawbridge started to rise. With a feat of unsurpassed horsemanship, he climbed to his feet and leapt from the saddle to the edge of the rising drawbridge. As his fingertips bit into the edge, the weight of the armour was too much to bear. Slowly releasing his grip on the wood, he looked down and said, "Oh well, so moat it be!"

•

### Kiss me quick . . .

Paddy was going home from the lodge meeting one evening, when a frog on the pavement called out to him and said, "If you kiss me, I'll turn into a beautiful princess."

Without a word, he bent over, picked up the frog and put it in his pocket. The creature spoke up again, louder this time, and said, "If you kiss me and turn me back into a beautiful princess, I will stay with you for a year and do anything you want."

Paddy took the frog out of his pocket, smiled at it and then returned it to the pocket. The frog then cried out desperately, "If you kiss me and turn me back into a princess, I'll stay with you forever and have your children!"

Again Paddy took the frog out, smiled at it benignly and put it back into his pocket.

Finally, the frog asked, with tears in its eyes, "What IS the matter? I've told you I'm a beautiful princess and that I'll stay with you forever and do anything you want.

WHY won't you kiss me?"

Paddy said, "Look, Oi'm a Master Mason. A girlfriend just takes up toime when I could be learning lectures. But a talking frog, now that will get me a free drink in the bar!"

•

"Goodness, Katie, be quiet!" scolded mummy. "Stop shouting like that. Be more like your little brother Tommy and play quietly."

"He's got to be quiet, Mummy. He's playing at being 'Daddy coming home from the Lodge'," said Katie.

"So why are you shouting?" asked mummy.

"Because I'm pretending to be you!"

•

Q: What's the difference between a Mason's wife and a wheelie bin?
A: The wheelie bin gets out once a week.

•

A businessman arrived home at eight in the morning. His wife, sitting at the breakfast table, angrily demanded where he'd been.

"I was working late with Janice, the new temp, and when we finished we went out for something to eat. We had a few drinks, a bottle of wine, and then went on to a club for a bit of a laugh and a few more drinks. Well, we ended up back at her flat and one thing led to another . . ."

"Don't lie to me. You were at that bloody Lodge again, weren't you?"

•

Jock was the foreman of a building site. He was sitting in his trailer when two bricklayers walked in.

"You'll have to do something about Jim," says one. "He's got a personal hygiene problem."

"He's a labourer lugging bricks around all day," said Jock. "Of course he's going to get a bit sweaty."

"Well, we're not working with him unless you do something about it!" the bricklayers replied before storming out.

So Jock calls Jim into the trailer and says, "There's no easy way to say this, so I'll just come straight to the point. B.O."

Jim appeared puzzled and replied, "A.Z."

"Get back to work, Jim," says Jock. "I've got to go and fire those two brickies."

•

Within a large town in America, there were three Masonic Lodges: Prince Hall, F & AM and AF & AM. All three had a serious problem with squirrel infestations in their buildings. Therefore, each Lodge, in its own fashion, had a special meeting to deal with the problem. The Prince Hall decided that the squirrels were predestined to be in the Lodge and that they would just have to live with them.

The F & AM decided they should deal with the squirrels in the movement's style of community responsibility and social action. They humanely trapped the animals and released them in a park on the edge of town, only to find that within three days, they had returned to the Lodge building.

The AF & AM Masonic Lodge had several lengthy special meetings, allowing all members to voice their opinions, and finally decided to have a secret ballot to vote the squirrels in as members of the Lodge. They now only see them during the PM night.

•

Ten Master Masons, happy, doing fine.
One listened to a rumour, then there were nine.

Nine Master Masons, faithful, never late.
One didn't like the Master, then there were eight.

Eight Master Masons, on their way to heaven.
One joined too many clubs, then there were seven.

Seven Master Masons, life dealt some hard licks.
One grew discouraged, then there were six.

Six Master Masons, all very much alive.
One lost his interest, then there were five.

Five Master Masons, wishing there were more.
Got into a great dispute, then there were four.

Four Master Masons, busy as could be.
One didn't like the programmes, then there were three.

Three Master Masons, was one of them you?
One grew tired of all the work, then there were two.

Two Master Masons with so much to be done.
One said "What's the use?", then there was one.

One Master Mason, found a Brother – (true!).
Brought him to the Lodge, then there were two.

Two Master Masons didn't find work a bore.
Each brought another, then there were four.

Four Master Masons saved their Lodge's fate.
By showing others kindness, then there were eight.

Eight Master Masons, loving their Lodge's bright sheen.
Talked so much about it, they soon counted sixteen.

Sixteen Master Masons, to their obligations true.
Were pleased when their number went to thirty-two.
If we can't put our troubles at the Lodge's door,
it's our own fault for harming the Lodge we adore.

Don't fuss about the programmes or the Master in the East.
Keep your obligation by serving even the very least.

•

A Mason went out to meetings a lot. "You never take me anywhere," his wife complained.
At 5.00 next morning, he woke her up and said, "Come to work with me!"

•

It seems a Jewish family had rented an apartment that sat directly under the Masonic Temple, and at least once a month they would always hear this stomping from above.
One day Jeremiah told his wife he was going to drill a hole in the ceiling and see what those Masons were up to. After doing so, one evening he heard some stomping coming from above, so he got his ladder, climbed up and decided to take a peek.
After a few moments, he flew down the ladder and ran in and told his wife to pack all their belongings. "Let's get out of here and fast!!!"
When she asked why, Jeremiah told her that he was just peeking in on the Masons above and saw them kill a man and said they were going to blame it on the "JEW BELOW".

•

# APPOINTED STEWARD

Q:  How were you first prepared to be made a Steward?

A:  My coat sleeves and shirt sleeves were rolled up and a corkscrew thrust into my hand.

Q:  What is a corkscrew?

A:  An implement fashioned like a winding staircase which our ancient Brethren ascended to receive their beer.

Q:  What is beer?

A:  A peculiar product of alchemy, veiled in mystery, and illustrated by labels.

Q:  How is it usually depicted in our assemblies?

A:  By a couple of hops near to a barrel of water.

Q:  Where did our ancient Brethren go to receive their beer?

A:  To a convivial room adjacent to the Lodge.

Q:  How did they receive it?

A:  In tankards and half tankards.

Q:  Why in this peculiar manner?

A:  In half tankards, well knowing that the same could easily be replenished and in tankards, from the great reliance that they placed on the mildness of the brew in those days.

Q:  What were the names of the two embellishments which decorated the doorway or entrance to this convivial room?

A:  That on the left was called 'Bass', and that on the right 'Guinness'.

Q:  What are their separate and conjoint significations?

A:  The former denotes 'strength', the latter 'sustenance' and when conjoined in a haphazard manner 'instability'. But when consumed without untoward excess they assist in promoting the spirit of friendship and harmony which should at all times characterise assemblies of Freemasons.

Q:  How many Masons does it take to change a light bulb?

A:  Seven - one to do the work and six Past Masters on the sidelines to prompt him.

•

## THE SIGN OF A MASON

A Mason was sitting with a number of non-Masons down at his local pub, where the landlord was also a Brother. Numerous jokes were cracked at the expense of the Fraternity, and the Mason was called upon to show them a Mason's sign. One of the men offered to give him a bottle of wine if he would comply with their wishes. At length, though with much apparent reluctance, he agreed, on the condition that the wine should be immediately produced, and that the individual consented to receive the communication privately.

The Mason added, "Friend, if you do not confess to the company that I have shown you a Freemason's sign, I will pay for the wine myself." The proposition was too reasonable to be refused, and the curious candidate for Masonic knowledge retired into another room with his friend. Once there the Mason asked, "So friend, you are curious to see a Freemason's sign and can you keep a secret?"

"Try me," said his friend.

"Good! You know that our friend Johnson, the pub landlord, is a Mason?"

"Yes, I do," he replied.

"Very well." Then taking him by the arm, the Mason led him to the window. "Do you see the painting of the lion hanging from the bracket on the wall?"

"Of course I do – it's our landlord's sign."

"Good!" replied the Mason. "Then friend, since our landlord is a Freemason, are you satisfied that I have shown you a Freemason's sign, and that the bottle of wine is forfeited? For your own sake, you will keep the secret."

The man returned to the room with a look of astonishment and confessed that he had received the desired information. He then turned to another of the cowans, whispering, "Do you want to see a sign of a Freemason? I'll show you for a bottle of wine."

•

## WHY MEN MAKE BETTER FRIENDS

### FRIENDSHIP BETWEEN WOMEN
A woman didn't come home one night. The next morning she told her husband that she had slept over at a friend's house. The man called his wife's ten best friends. None of them knew anything about it.

### FRIENDSHIP BETWEEN MEN
A man didn't come home one night. The next morning he told his wife that he had slept over at a friend's house. The woman called her husband's ten best friends, eight of whom confirmed that he had slept over, and two said that he was still there.

•

A certain Right Worshipful Sir was speeding down the road when he looked in his rear view mirror and saw the dreaded flashing lights. As he drove on he realised the policeman wanted to stop him, so he pulled over to the hard shoulder of the highway. The young policeman walked up to the driver's door and the RW Sir realised that to compound matters not only was he speeding, he was not wearing his seat belt. Whooommmp! On went the seat belt. The policeman knocked on the window and the RW Sir lowered the window.

The officer said, "Good evening, RW Sir. Late for a Masonic meeting?"

The RW Sir thought to himself, "This young man knows me, I don't know him, but I may get out of this ticket."

"Ah, mmm! Yes, I am quite late. I should have been there 15 minutes ago."

The young policeman said, "RW Sir, I clocked you at 75mph in a 55mph limit, but I am willing to let you off the ticket if you can answer but one question for me."

The RW Sir thought to himself, "I have been Chairman of Education for a number of years. I should be able to answer any question this young man has."

"Go ahead, ask me anything."

The policeman said, "Tell me RW Sir, do you find it difficult to steer the car with your seat belt through the steering wheel?"

•

An ambitious yuppie finally decided to take a holiday. He booked himself on a Caribbean cruise and proceeded to have the time of his life - at least for a while. A hurricane came unexpectedly. The ship went down and was lost instantly. The man found himself swept up on the shore of an island with no other people, no supplies, nothing. Only bananas and coconuts. Used to four-star hotels, this guy had no idea what to do. So for the next four months he ate bananas, drank coconut juice, longed for his old life and fixed his gaze on the sea, hoping to spot a rescue ship.

One day, as he was lying on the beach, he spotted movement out of the corner of his eye. It was a rowing boat, and in it was the most gorgeous woman he had ever seen. She rowed up to him.

In disbelief, he asked her: "Where did you come from? How did you get here?"

"I rowed from the other side of the island," she said. "I landed here when my cruise ship sank."

"Amazing," he said, "I didn't know anyone else had survived. How many of you are there? You were really lucky that a rowing boat washed up with you."

"It's only me," she said, "and the rowing boat didn't wash up; nothing did."

He was confused, "Then how did you get the rowing boat?"

"Oh, simple," replied the woman. "I made it out of raw material that I found on the island. The oars were whittled from gum tree branches, I wove the bottom from palm branches, and the sides and stern came from a eucalyptus tree."

"But, but, that's impossible," stuttered the man. "You had no tools or hardware; how did you manage?"

"Oh, that was no problem," the woman said. "On the south side of the island, there is a very unusual stratum of exposed alluvial rock. I found that if I fired it to a certain temperature in my kiln, it melted into forgeable ductile iron. I used that for tools, and used the tools to make the hardware. But enough of that. Where do you live?"

Sheepishly, the man confessed that he had been sleeping on the beach the whole time.

"Well, let's row over to my place, then," she said. After a few minutes of rowing, she docked the boat at a small wharf. As the man looked to the shore, he nearly fell out of the boat. Before him was a stone path leading to an exquisite bungalow painted in blue and white. While the woman tied up the rowing boat with an expertly woven hemp rope, the man could only stare ahead, dumbstruck.

As they walked into the house, she said casually, "It's not much, but I call it home. Sit down, please. Would you like to have a drink?"

"No, no, thank you," he said, still dazed. "I can't take any more coconut juice."

"It's not coconut juice," the woman replied. "I have a still. How about a pina colada?"

Trying to hide his continued amazement, the man accepted, and they sat down on her couch to talk.

After they had exchanged their stories, the woman announced, "I'm going to slip into something more comfortable. Would you like to take a shower and shave? There is a razor upstairs in the cabinet in the bathroom."

No longer questioning anything, the man went into the bathroom. There in the cabinet was a razor made from a bone handle. Two shells honed to a hollow ground edge were fastened to its tip, inside a swivel mechanism. "This woman is amazing," he mused. "What next?"

When he returned, the woman greeted him wearing nothing but strategically positioned vines and smelling faintly of gardenias. She beckoned for him to sit down next to her. "Tell me," she began suggestively, slithering closer to him, "We've been out here for a very long time. You've been lonely. There's something I'm sure you really feel like doing right now, something you"ve been longing for all these months? You know. . . ." She stared into his eyes.

He couldn't believe what he was hearing: "You mean. . ." he replied, "I can check my e-mail and the Freemason-List from here?"

·

A Freemason parks his brand new Porsche in front of the Lodge to show it off to his Brethren.

As he gets out of the car, a lorry races along too close to the kerb and takes off the door before speeding off.

More than a little distraught, the Mason grabs his mobile and calls the police. Five minutes later, the police arrive. He starts screaming hysterically, "My Porsche, my beautiful red Porsche is ruined. No matter how long it takes at the panel beaters, it'll simply never be the same again!"

After the Brother finally finishes his rant, the policeman shakes his head in disgust: "I can't believe how materialistic you bloody Masons are. You lot are so focused on your possessions that you don't notice anything else in your life."

"How can you say such a thing at a time like this?" snaps the Brother.

The policeman replies, "Didn't you realise that your right arm was torn off when the lorry hit you?"

The Brother looks down in absolute horror, "Bloody Hell!" he screams. "Where's my Rolex?"

·

A very eminent Brother was driving along a busy street in London when, ahead of him, a traffic light changed to red. The car in front stopped at the line and he dutifully took his place in the queue.

The lights changed to green and expecting to pull away any second, our VW Brother slipped the car into gear and hung on the handbrake. From the car in front? Nothing, it didn't even move an inch.

Being a patient soul, the VWB waited and waited and eventually the lights returned to red. Not wishing to be stuck at the lights a moment longer, the second the lights went to green again, the VWB leant on the horn, when he was affronted by an arm out of the window in front with a middle finger stabbing the air.

He thought to himself, "I'm not putting up with that kind of rudeness, I'll have a word with the bastard." He opened the door, got out and strode towards the car in front. On drawing level with the car, he looked in and saw a little blue book on the seat next to the driver and said, "I acknowledge the correctness of the sign!"

•

Q:    How many Masons does it take to change a light bulb?
A:    Two. One to search for the light and one to raise him up.

•

## MASONIC CRITICISM

We know that in the character of a Master Mason, you are authorised to correct the errors and irregularities of your uninformed Brethren and to guard them against a breach of fidelity. But before criticising a Brother, take heed of that old adage and never criticise another until you have walked a mile in his shoes. There are two good reasons for this. Firstly if he gets mad at your criticism, you'll be a mile away. And secondly, you've got his shoes.

•

## SICKNESS AND DISTRESS

When the Master asked about cases of sickness and distress, it was reported that the Brother who had fallen into the upholstery machine was now completely recovered.

•

## BROTHERLY ADVICE

"My Brother," said the old Past Master to the newly raised Master Mason, "There are two secrets to success in life: Number 1. Never tell people everything you know…"

•

## MASONIC FUNERAL SERVICES

In every Lodge or District there is always one faithful Brother who officiates at most of the Masonic funeral services. This story may be modified to fit him.

The local Funeral Director phoned the old Brother who always performed the Masonic funeral services and said he needed his help. It seemed that a body had been shipped in from out of state with the instructions that a Masonic graveside service be performed, and nothing more. The departed Brother had no family or friends in the area, and was to be buried in a small graveyard far out in the country that very day. The faithful Brother said he would be glad to provide a Masonic service for this Brother, so he put on his black suit, stuck a sprig of evergreen in his breast pocket, and headed out to the cemetery. He had never been there before, and the instructions provided by the Funeral Director were not too clear, so he soon found himself lost. After driving up and down miles and miles of dirt roads, he finally arrived about 45 minutes late. By that time, the hearse was nowhere in sight and the vault was closed. The workmen were leaning up against the backhoe, in the shade of a tree, eating their lunch. Faithful to his trust, the old Brother advanced to the head of the grave, alone, and proceeded to deliver one of the best graveside services that he had ever done. As he was making his way back to his car, feeling happy about what he had been able to do, one of the workmen said to another, "Well, I ain't never seen anything like that before, and I've been puttin' in these septic tanks for 20 years."

•

A new Mason was constantly reviewing his EA work in preparation for his examination. He gave no thought to reciting this in front of his five-year-old daughter. One day while in the bathroom he heard a knock on the door and he immediately asked, "Who comes here?" The five year old responded, "A poor blind candidate and I need to pee."

•

A Mason was at work for the Post Office during the Christmas season. He noticed a letter addressed to Santa Claus. After a few minutes of study, he thought it wouldn't be against the rules to open a letter to Santa. The letter was from a woman who said she was a single mother and would he please send her £500 to buy presents for her children. The postman carried the letter to Lodge with him and they collected £400 which they appointed a committee to deliver in time for the mother to buy her children the presents. A few days later the postman again noticed a letter addressed to Santa and it was from the same address as the single mother. He promptly opened the letter which said, "Santa I really appreciate the money you sent me for my children, but next time please send it by someone else. The Masons kept £100 of it."

•

Two drunken Glaswegians staggered out of a pub in search of additional pintage when one got the idea to investigate the local Masonic lodge. "They've always got extra bevy in they places!" the first one said.

"But dae ye not haftae know wan o' they secret handshakes?" asked the second.

"You leave that tae me, pal! Nae bother!" replied the first, confidently.

The first old Scotsman strode up the hill towards the Lodge, only to come tumbling back down a few minutes later, clutching his face in obvious pain.

"What the devil happened, Jock? Could ye no' get us in?" asked the friend.

"I don't know what happened, Angus! There was a big strappin' laddie outside the front door. He asked me if I was a Mason, and I said yes. Then he said, "Bo," and I said "Peep," and the bugger broke my nose!"

•

Brother Jones was just installed as the Worshipful Master of his Lodge. It was a cold night as he walked the four blocks to his home on that special night. He kept thinking of how his Brothers had paid so much respect to him on his elevation to that high office. It was his proudest moment as a Mason and he was now an installed leader of the Craft!

His wife had already gone to bed, so he was careful not to wake her as he slowly slid under the warm blankets. As careful as he was, his foot touched his wife's leg, waking her. She shouted "God, your feet are cold!" He responded, "Sorry sweetheart, but you can still call me honey."

•

My favourite masonic joke is about the Entered Apprentice who knew too much. When he was asked why the North was a place of darkness, he answered that it's because that's where the Past Masters take their naps.

•

Q: How many Masons does it take to change a light bulb?
A: None. A Mason doesn't change a light. Masonic Light changes the man.

•

It was an exciting day for Freemasonry in Dublin. One of the Past Masters of the Lodge was appearing on the television quiz show Mastermind. His specialist subject: Freemasonry and its history. The questions started:

When was the Bail Bridge Square discovered?
"Pass."
When was the first Grand Lodge founded?
"Pass."
Who was the first Irish Grand Master?
"Pass."

Then a voice from the crowd piped up,
"That's right, Paddy, don't you tell him nothing!"

•

The Festive Board is not only enjoyable for the food but also for the humour that is so often a feature of the toasts one hears on those occasions. On one such instance when an English Brother was a visitor to a Barbados Lodge a native Barbadian Brother was nominated to propose a toast to him. He began by saying that when Barbadians are born, they are born black; when out in the sun, they remain black; and when they die, they die black!

But when an Englishman is born, he is born pink; when he is frightened, he turns white; when he is hot, he goes red; when he is cold, he goes blue; when he is ill, he turns green; when he is jaundiced, he goes yellow; when out in the sun, he goes brown; when enraged, he goes purple; and when he dies, he goes grey. So the one thing the Brother said he could never understand about the English is why they call the Barbadians coloured!

•

The funniest thing happened when we were getting a very nervous Army Officer ready to go into the Lodge. We asked him to salute the WM as a Mason. The next thing we knew he stamped his foot and gave a very smart military salute, with his hand quivering at his forehead.

•

Shortly before Christmas, three elderly Brethren were called to the Grand Lodge Above. On arrival at the Pearly Gates they were met by the Tyler (St Peter). They were greeted well, but informed that due to a considerable amount of crowding at this time of year they would have to produce from about their person an item connected with Christmas to gain admission.

The first Brother felt in his pockets and produced a cigarette lighter. "What has that got to do with Christmas?" asked St. Peter. The Brother flicked the lighter into life and declared it was like a Christmas candle.

"You may enter Brother."

The second Brother produced a bunch of keys. "And what relevance does that have to Christmas?" asked St Peter. The Brother shook the keys and said they were like Jingle Bells. He too was granted admission.

The third Brother then delved deep into his pockets and finally, with some embarrassment, produced a pair of very frilly knickers. Not surprisingly St Peter was somewhat astonished by this item and said, "What in Heaven's name has that got to do with Christmas?" The Brother, looking somewhat sheepish, replied, "They're Carol's!"

●

Two young Master Masons were driving home from an Installation Meeting at a Lodge some 200 miles from where they lived. Around midnight, in the middle of a snowstorm, they decided it was too dangerous to drive any further. So they pulled into a nearby farm and asked the attractive lady who answered the door if they could spend the night.

"I realise the weather's terrible out there and I have this huge house all to myself, but I'm recently widowed," she explained. "I'm afraid the neighbours will talk if I let you stay in my house."

"Don't worry," Jack said. "We'll be happy to sleep in the barn. And as soon as the weather improves we'll be gone." The lady agreed, and the two Masons found their way to the barn and settled in for the night. Come morning, the weather had cleared and they got on their way and, as neither of them were married, there were no problems or explanations required when they got home. About nine months later, Jack got an unexpected letter from a solicitor. It took him a few minutes to work it out, but he finally determined that it was from the widow's solicitor.

He dropped in on his friend Bob and asked, "Bob, do you remember that good-looking widow from the farm we stayed at when we were caught in the snow about nine months ago?"

"Yes, I do," said Bob.

"Did you, er, happen to get up in the middle of the night, go up to the house and pay her a visit?"

"Well, um, yes," Bob said, a little embarrassed about being found out. "I have to admit that I did."

"And did you happen to give her my name instead of telling her yours?"

Bob's face turned bright red and he said, "Yeah; look I'm sorry, mate. I'm afraid I did. Why do you ask?"

"She's just died and left me everything."

•

President Barack Obama is visiting a Glasgow hospital.

He enters a ward full of patients with no
obvious sign of injury or illness. He greets one.
The patient replies:

"Fair fa' your honest, sonsie face,
    Great chieftain o' the puddin-race!
Aboon them a' ye tak yer place,
    Painch, tripe, or thairm:

Weel are ye wordy of a grace
    As lang's my arm."

President Obama is confused, so he just grins
and moves on to the next patient.
The next patient responds:

"Some hae meat an canna eat,
    And some wad eat that want it,
But we hae meat an' we can eat,
    Sae let the Lord be thankit."

Even more confused, and his grin now rictus-like,
the President moves onto the next patient,
who immediately begins to chant:

"Wee, sleekit, cow'rin, tim'rous beastie,
    O, what a panic's in thy breastie!
Thou need na start awa sae hasty,
    Wi bickering brattle!"

Now seriously troubled, Obama turns to the
accompanying doctor and asks,
"Is this a psychiatric ward?'"
"No," replies the doctor,
"this is the serious Burns unit."

•

A ragged tramp stopped a Mason on his way home from the lodge and asked him for money for food.

"I'll do better than that!" said the Mason. "Come into the pub, and I'll buy you a drink!"

"Thank you!" said the beggar. "But I've never drunk and I never will!"

"Well, let me buy you some cigarettes then!" said the Mason.

"No, thanks!" said the tramp, "I've never smoked and I never will!"

"Okay," said the Mason. "Come back to the Lodge with me and I'll see you get a meal!"

"No, thanks," said the man. "I've never entered a Masonic Lodge and I never will!"

"Right, then", said the Mason. "Will you please come home with me and meet my wife!" "Why?" asked the tramp.

"Well," said the Mason, "I just want her to see what happens to a guy who doesn't drink, doesn't smoke and hasn't joined the Masons!"

•

A young EA came running into the WM's robing room, shouting, "WM, there is a case of Syphilis in the Lodge."

The WM replied, "Thank goodness for that, I was getting sick of Beaujolais!"

•

Do you know a Masonic joke that should be included in the next edition?

Why not email it to us at jokes@lewismasonic.com